LIKING MYSELF
LOVING MY LIFE

21 DAYS TO ENJOYING RIGHT NOW

NANCEY WEST

Copyright @ 2021 Nancey West

All quoted Scripture is from THE HOLY BIBLE, NEW INTERNATIONAL VERSION®, NIV® Copyright © 1973, 1978, 1984, 2011 by Biblica, Inc.® Used by permission.
All rights reserved worldwide

ISBN: 9798723604728

All rights reserved

No part of this publication may be reproduced, distributed, or transmitted in any form or by any means, including photocopying, recording, or other electronic or mechanical methods, without the prior written permission of the publisher, except in the case of brief quotations embodied in reviews and certain other non-commercial uses permitted by copyright law.

West Publishing

170 Grant St. Lebanon, OR 97355

Dedication

To all the women who have struggled to find peace with who they are.

Table of Contents

Foreword 9

Introduction 11

Day 1:
Inherent Value 23

Day 2:
Believing in Your Value 27

Day 3:
Positive Energy 29

Day 4:
Self-Talk 33

Day 5:
Overwhelmed 37

Day 6:
Labels 41

Day 7:
Expectations 45

Day 8:
Your Past 49

Day 9:
Forgiveness 53

Day 10:
Distorted Thoughts 57

Day 11:
Victim Mindset 61

Day 12:
Triggers 65

Day 13:
Boundaries 69

Day 14:
Today's Decisions, Tomorrow's Dreams..................73

Day 15:
Comparing 77

Day 16:
Competition 81

Day 17:
Sabotaging Yourself 85

Day 18:
Supporting Others 89

Day 19:
Gratitude 93

Day 20:
Design Your Future 97

Day 21:
Sow into Your Life 101

Special Thanks 109

Resources 111

About the Author.. 113

Thank You Gift

Thank you so much for choosing **Liking Myself. Loving My Life**. I hope, pray and fully expect that this book will be a tremendous blessing to you.

As a Thank You, I would love to share with you the companion **Tool Kit & Planning Guide** that I've put together to accompany this book. That's where you'll find helpful prompts and instructions to help retrain your brain to like the woman in the mirror. Please visit http://www.nanceywest.com/gift to grab your free copy.

Blessings,
Nancey West

Foreword

They told me God loved me.

And I thought to myself, "That's nice. I'm pretty sure that's His job." But I never really believed that God liked me. Because frankly, I didn't like myself, and no one else seemed to like me, either.

Then something happened. The specific details of the circumstance are long forgotten. But I had once again been rejected in a way that left me overwhelmed with self-loathing.

As I sat in church one Sunday morning, feeling alone in the crowd, I felt the God of the universe reach down and touch me. And I heard him speak to my heart in a way that was so clear, it felt like He was sitting next to me. I'll never forget the words, "I like you, Donna. I like you just the way you are."

I've wasted many years not liking myself. That's why I'm so excited about this inspiring and super-practical book by Nancey West. Drawing on her own life experience and the latest research about how to form new mental habits, she's mapped out a 21-day transformational program for Christian women.

It may seem strange to buy a "loving myself book." But the truth is if you love God and want to show love to others, breaking free of low self-esteem is a great place to begin. People who love God and others are at peace with themselves, not consumed by debilitating self-hatred.

I love the promise of this book: at the end of the journey, you'll be able to look in the mirror and like the person looking back at you. God likes you, and He wants you to like you, too.

You can start liking yourself and loving your life. You can begin enjoying today right now. This book by Nancey West will show you the way.

Donna Partow

Million-Copy Bestselling Author, ***Becoming the Woman God Wants Me To Be***

Introduction

Have you ever felt worthless? I mean like you were *wasting air* kind of worthless? You thought God made a mistake when He created you. You didn't fit in and you surely weren't going anywhere. I used to believe that. You don't have to.

Are you ready to stop being your own worst enemy... and start becoming your own best friend? Good, I'm glad to hear it!

You weren't born with distorted thinking. You weren't born with destructive thoughts about how life *always turns out for you*. You developed patterns of thinking and feeling in response to your life experiences.

I know because I spent years searching for answers to "what good am I?" I stumbled my way through life in constant emotional pain. But by God's grace, I went from *feeling* like I was completely worthless to *knowing* I am utterly priceless. You can too.

You don't have to take decades like I did. You can face whatever's holding you back and start to change all of that beginning right now.

In 21 days, I will show you areas where you need to adjust your thinking so you can become the woman you want to be. Together, we'll make those adjustments, little by little, a day at a time. The process will seem almost effortless...and yet it's so very powerful!

You probably aren't even aware of the way you talk to yourself right now. But chances are, it's mostly negative. In fact, researchers have found that 80% of all self-talk is negative. If you're anything like I was, it's more like 100% *down-on-yourself*. Trust me, you're going to feel much better about yourself, and about life, when you develop the habit of positive self-talk.

And that's exactly what it is: a habit. And habits can change. That means YOU can change. Isn't that good to know?

Do you want to walk into a room and feel confident? Do you want to improve your relationships? Are you ready to look in the mirror and genuinely *like* the woman staring back at you? It can happen. I'm here to help.

Life doesn't remain stagnant. If you aren't working toward improving how you relate to yourself, your life isn't going to get any better on its own. Next year you will be a year older. You'll either be a *better* person or a *more bitter* one. But for sure, you won't stay the same.

It's time to get rid of the lies you have believed about yourself. Follow this system and soon you'll see yourself as the cherished woman God intended you to be.

Have you looked in the mirror lately? I mean really looked. Not to find fault. You need to look in the mirror and tell that person just how important she is. Don't look away. I know the tricks. You are telling yourself I am not talking to you. But I am! Look her in the eyes and smile. After all, she isn't going anywhere. You can keep her as an enemy...or turn her into a friend. It's up to you.

Hold your mirror up. Whoa, that is too close to your face. You aren't examining every flaw. You are looking at the lovely woman others see. Don't zoom in on your imperfections. Don't let tiny blemishes magnify into giant faults. Forget that. Look for the things you can cheer about.

I spent too many years focusing on the flaws. Yeah, that was me. Every situation, every gathering, sometimes even when I was alone, I thought about what I looked like. What others thought of me. How could I hide? I didn't want people looking at me. I just wanted to be a wallflower, observing life and not participating. Actually, that's exactly what I was. I cowered out-of-sight whenever possible.

I found so many flaws that I began to really dislike myself. I searched for something positive. Nope, I couldn't find anything. I only saw the distorted images I thought were true.

One day, I had just botched a job interview and was wondering what was next. I was thinking, "Why go on?" I stood in front of the mirror and stared at the red, swollen eyes and beet-red cheeks. I grabbed a bottle of pills I had recently received from a doctor to help me lose weight. I choked down the entire bottle. I again looked in the mirror, threw the remainder of the water in the glass at the mirror, and with my heart breaking, I screamed, "I HATE YOU! I HATE YOU! I HATE YOU!"

Then I curled up on my bed and waited for the pills to take effect. There was no pain. I just got very tired. My roommate came home unexpectedly and took me to the hospital.

People make jokes and have pat answers on why someone would try to take their own life. *They feel sorry for themselves. They want attention.* Simple explanations that don't address the real problem. I wanted to show everyone that I didn't like myself any better than I thought anyone else did.

I wanted someone to hold me and say I was worthwhile. I craved a hug or a pat on the back. Boy, it would be nice if someone said I was valuable. Actually, I just wanted to be a normal person, but I didn't even know what that really meant.

Ok, take a fresh look in that mirror. What reaction do you have? Do you see a smiling face staring back? Look again. Sit up, back straight, shoulders square, and with a strong, affirmative voice say, "I like myself."

You might feel ridiculous at first. But I promise, it's going to get easier. By the time you reach the end of this book, you'll be able to say it and mean it.

You... no matter what you have done, no matter what you have been through, no matter what...can learn to see yourself in a new way. You can like yourself. And you can love your life.

- Stop looking in the mirror and comparing yourself with photo-shopped images.

- Stop looking in the mirror just to find fault *(examining every wart)*.

- Stop looking in the mirror with your eyes fixed on what's behind you *(the people who once hurt you)*.

- Stop letting what you see right now block your vision of what's ahead. Let yourself look beyond the present to see a brighter future ahead.

We are going to change the way you look in the mirror so you can see and enjoy that incredible person.

This book will help you identify areas where you may not realize that you are creating your own roadblocks. Each day we will discuss one area. We will look at symptoms you may relate to and ways to get rid of bad habits. Spend time pondering how each issue relates to you. Dig deep. Keep a journal so you can review your thoughts.

Don't let your life pass you by. You need to start Enjoying Right Now. You're about to learn exactly how.

Your Daily Mirror Time

Over the next 21 days, you are going to retrain your brain using a scientifically-proven strategy, based on research into addictive behaviors by Stanford University professor, B.J. Fogg, author of **Tiny Habits: The Small Changes that Change Everything**. You are going to teach your brain to like you...and to love your life. In fact, you are going to *get addicted* to being nice to yourself.

And it's going to be FUN, I promise!

Take this book with you to wherever you brush your teeth each morning. If you can do this right now, that's ideal. If you're not home, set an alarm or reminder on your phone to do this as soon as you walk in your front door.

Now pick up your toothbrush. You're going to brush your teeth. I don't care if you just brushed them before picking up this book. I want you to brush them again. With the toothbrush *still in your hand*, I want you to look in the mirror, look yourself right in the eye and finish this sentence three times in a row:

I like myself right now because _____

Give three good reasons why you like yourself at this moment. Think of three things you did right today and give yourself some credit.

Some examples might include:

- I like myself right now because I bought a copy of **Liking Myself, Loving My Life** and I'm already **Enjoying Right Now**.

- I like myself right now because I did a nice job with my eyeshadow today.

- I like myself right now because I was nice to the lady at the store, even though she was grumpy toward me.

It doesn't really matter what you come up with to like about yourself. Just remember to finish the sentence three times in a row.

Next, finish this sentence three times in a row:

I love my life right now because _____

You can share anything you love about your life (your circumstances and the people around you, etc). Some examples might include:

- I love my life right now because I live in a world with toothbrushes and good dental care.

- I love my life right now because I have a roof over my head and a warm bed to sleep in.

- I love my life right now because I have at least one true friend.

For more sample prompts for these two exercises, you can get a free copy of the daily companion Tool Kit at www.NanceyWest.com/gift.

The important thing is to do this exercise every day, while the toothbrush is still in your hand, before you put it back wherever it belongs. This is what Dr. Fogg calls a "Prompt" – something in your environment that signals a habit to unfold. Let your toothbrush *prompt you* to do your new Daily Mirror Time habit each morning and evening...whenever you brush your teeth.

Never miss! It only takes a minute, so don't skip it. You are forming a new habit. You are retraining your brain to *like you* and be nice to you.

To reinforce your new habit, you can grab an erasable white board marker and scribble a reminder on your mirror. You can even use lipstick. Lots of women do! Or you can grab a post-it note, write "Mirror Time" and stick it next to your toothbrush.

If you use your phone or Alexa for reminders, set up reminders on those devices, as well. You can even do all of the above so if one Prompt doesn't do the trick, another one will. Do whatever it takes to remind yourself to begin and stick to this habit. It's going to revolutionize your life.

And now there's one more scientific "hack" to help make this habit stick. It's going to sound silly, but it's proven to work. If you've ever played Candy Crush (or similar online apps) just for fun...then gradually realized you were addicted, that was no accident. It was by design.

And guess who came up with the design? Right, students trained by B.J. Fogg to create addictive games and Facebook apps – not to mention Instagram.

In fact, Dr. Fogg felt so guilty about all the people he had helped get addicted to worthless online nonsense that he decided to write **Tiny Habits**. His goal is to help people like you and me develop positive habits. And that's exactly what we're going to do with our Daily Mirror Time.

Now here's the big secret: mini-celebration.

Yes, I said celebration. Let me guess. You thought I was going to say motivation or self-discipline were top priorities. Nope. Not according to the world's leading expert on habit formation.

We change best when we *feel good* about ourselves. We change best when we feel like *success is possible* for us.

Not when we set unrealistic goals. Not when we *set ourselves up for failure*. Been there done that. This is a new day and a new way.

That's exactly what mini-celebration is designed to accomplish. By celebrating small wins, you gradually convince your brain that YOU are capable of winning. That you are, in fact, a winner.

You can cultivate the learned skill of *making yourself feel good*.

In the past, if you're anything like me, you just passively hoped for someone or something outside of you to make you feel good.

Those days are gone. Beginning right now, you are in charge of *making yourself feel good* about yourself and about your life. You're going to start building what psychologists call "emotional resilience" – the ability to bounce back when life knocks you down.

And you do it by celebrating yourself and giving yourself credit where credit is due. As of today, your mini-celebration strategy is your way of defying society's unrealistic expectations and instead, congratulating yourself for every baby step you take forward.

Go you! You're a rock star!

You might feel silly celebrating yourself. You might be tempted to skip it. But mini-celebration is scientifically-proven to work and, according to Dr. Fogg, if you want to change your life and you can only change one thing, then this is the one thing you have to change.

Did you know that the Bible commands us 88 times to celebrate? The book of Nehemiah commands the people to *"celebrate with great joy"* (Nehemiah 8:12). God knew how we were made long before Stanford University figured it out.

It's time to start celebrating. What exactly do I mean by mini-celebration? Here are some examples:

- Smile at yourself
- Pump your fists in the air
- Hum the Rocky Theme Song
- Do a little dance
- Sing a line from an inspirational song
- Shout, "I'm a Rockstar" or "Go me!"
- Throw your hands in the air and declare, "VICTO-RY" or "Nailed it!"
- Clap your hands
- Blow a kiss at yourself
- Curtsy to yourself like you're royalty
- Give yourself two thumbs up

If you're not sure which mini-celebration strategy is right for you, imagine you just received a text or email with the best news you've heard in years.

What do you instantly do?

If you follow sports, how do you celebrate when your team scores a goal or wins the game? Those are great clues to your natural celebration style. You can try a variety of mini-celebration approaches until you find the one that "fits" you best.

So here's the proven formula you're going to follow to get addicted to being nice to yourself over the next 21 days:

- **After** I brush my teeth
- **I will** have my Daily Mirror Time.
- **To celebrate**, I will _____

I know you can do it. You are not reading this book by mistake. It's not an accident. God not only loves you, He likes you. And He wants you to like you, too. That journey begins in 3.2.1...

I like myself right now because _____ , I love my life right now because _____.

I like myself right now because I'm writing these words for you. I love my life right now because God has given me the privilege of inviting you into a whole new way of living. Go me!

Check the box when you are done:

☐ I like myself (3x)

☐ I love my life (3x)

Now celebrate that you have chosen to begin this journey! Go and enjoy right now!

Day 1:
Inherent Value

Let's dive in. Hold your mirror up. It may be cracked, or maybe you have plastered it with mud, and you can't see that beautiful image clearly. Smile, and let's clean the mirror for a realistic view.

You have a God-given value, but you may have covered it up beneath shovel after shovel of doubt, fear, and neglect. You may have started with a small amount of anger, then negative connotations from others, and by the time you threw on some hateful name-calling, you can hardly see your worth. A few more shovel-loads of rejection and all sight of the value God gave you is lost. But you didn't stop shoveling, did you? You heaped on more self-condemnation, uncertainty, and guilt and forgot what you had buried. Your value never changed. It is just hidden beneath the damage you have experienced.

Do you think I was worthless when I attempted to take my life? No, God saw the child He loved. He saw the years of pain that grew with each lie I believed. You are just as valuable as I am. And He loves you just as much.

DAY 1: INHERENT VALUE

You are perfect in God's eyes, formed and shaped to be uniquely yourself. You are God's treasure, worth so much more than you can imagine.

"Consider the ravens: They do not sow or reap; they have no storeroom or barn, yet God feeds them. And how much more valuable are you than birds" (Luke 12:24). Don't fool yourself by thinking that God is not concerned about you. He hurts each time you criticize yourself. He sees that original value because it is still there. He loves you through the rejection, abuse, deceit, or whatever the world has thrown at you. To God, you shine as brightly as you did when He created you.

When God created man, He said, *"It was very good"* (Genesis 1:31 NIV). When Adam and Eve chose to eat of the fruit of good and evil, their original value did not change. Sin brought brokenness, but it did not reduce the acceptance and love God had for us. We are still His delight. *"This is love; not that we loved God, but that he loved us"* (1 John 4:10).

Have you ever felt worthless? That is a terrible feeling and one you don't have to carry. Someone made you feel that way. Someone's actions, or even your own, will not diminish your value. Who is burying your value? What are you doing to bury it? Are you ready to dig it up?

The thing is, you need to accept the truth of your own worth. You need to recognize the crack in the mirror that is falsely telling you who you are. See yourself as your Creator does.

Are you better off living with your image seen in a muddy, cracked mirror? Or would you prefer to bask in the warmth of your true value? Did you get some of the mirror washed off so you can enjoy that beautiful image?

Think about who you really are, accept it, and claim it every day. Remind yourself that you have inherent value right now, and it can't be taken away!

It is important that you do something to celebrate. You need to remind your brain to celebrate every time you turn a distorted thought into a truthful one; every time you turn an unrealistic perspective into a realistic one; or any time you do something good for yourself. And your brain remembers best with an action added to it. Reward yourself with some kind of gesture. Even if it is a smile in the mirror and a nod of your head. Do something to acknowledge that you are making progress. No matter how small the achievement, you need to feel that spark of warmth inside that you did it. A small spark will become a flame when you keep it going.

If you remind your brain often enough, it will begin reminding you. Your heart likes that warm, fuzzy feeling created when celebrating and will want to come back to it. Find something you do naturally when you are cheering for a child, grandchild or a team. Use that action to celebrate yourself.

Smile at yourself in the mirror. That is an accomplishment. Reward yourself with a thumbs up. There, you have started your celebration routine. The more you succeed, the bigger you may want to make the celebration. What do you do when you celebrate? Cheer? Dance? High-five? Fist-pump? Whatever makes you feel like a winner. Start practicing so you can cheer yourself on after every day when you tackle another problem.

DAY 1: INHERENT VALUE

Don't forget, you are worth every effort you put into liking yourself.

When I am excited, I say aloud, "I'm doing my happy-dance on the inside." My body doesn't wiggle much, but my heart bubbles over.

Look in the mirror and celebrate your reclaimed value, saying:

I like myself right now because _____, I love my life right now because _____.

Check the box when you are done:

☐ I like myself (3x)

☐ I love my life (3x)

Having inherent value is awesome. Celebrate right now!

Day 2:
Believing in Your Value

Fortune cookies don't have much value, but they can offer something to think about. One message I pulled from a crispy cookie said, "He loves you as much as he can, but he can't love you very much."

As humans, we have a limit in our capacity to love. Your experience shapes your ability to love and be loved. If you felt rejected early in life, you may be afraid of intimacy and trust. If you felt unloved or misunderstood, you may be defensive and unable to accept or express love.

The fear of being hurt can build a barrier for self-protection, while the desire for love makes you vulnerable to the pain of rejection—a confusing situation for sure.

God's love fulfills us. So why wasn't I fulfilled during those years before I gave up and tried to take my life? I knew God's love in my head. However, I was looking for validation from people. I was seeking human love, which is conditional and limited. I ignored God's love,

DAY 2: BELIEVING IN YOUR VALUE

which is unconditional and everlasting. I wanted someone to tell me I was okay, that I mattered.

Look in your mirror. How do you feel about this person that God loves?

This person looking back from the mirror is the one you need to be friends with. Best friends would be even better. That person needs to be someone you can spend time alone with and be content and comfortable with, someone you can laugh with, dream with and even argue with. That person is with you wherever you go, so you might as well enjoy the company.

You can turn self-disdain to self-love with your focus. Who are you focused on? You can concentrate on your own pain until it solidifies into a prison. Or you can accept God's love and guidance, knowing He cares for you. Do you know what "cares" means? He does what is best for you! *"I will heal their waywardness and love them freely"* (Hosea 14:4). Focus on that.

Take another look in the mirror. Is your image any clearer? We will clean some more mud off tomorrow. For now, show me your celebration reaction! Look in the mirror and say to your new best friend, I like myself right now because _____, I love my life right now because _____. Add a beat to it. Have fun with it.

Check the box when you are done:

- ☐ I like myself (3x)
- ☐ I love my life (3x)

Go and enjoy now! Celebrate the seeking and growing person you are right now! Are you starting to feel that warmth inside?

Day 3:

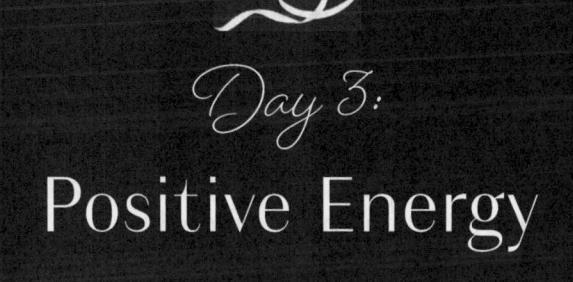

Positive Energy

You reap what you sow.

That statement always made me feel like whatever happened to me was my fault. Someone would mistreat me because I first did something to them, or they perceived that I had done something. I caused them to react in the way they did.

I believed that lie for years. We don't cause people to react. People choose how they will react. That includes you and me. We decide how we will respond in situations. Feelings are fickle. They can change anytime. If you don't want your emotions to take over and run amuck, you need to make a plan. Think about how you will react in a given situation.

Take control of your natural and sometimes justified emotions to get control of your future. You have a built-in default that takes you to survival mode: defenses up, ready for the attack. That usually leads to a negative outcome.

Do you consider yourself a person with a positive attitude? Or a negative attitude?

Do you pay attention to the good rather than the bad in people or situations?

Or do you ignore the good and go straight to finding fault?

The type of thoughts you choose will determine your day and shape your reality. Your attitude may not change the situation, but it will change how you see what is happening and how you decide.

In the past, when someone would disagree with me, I felt that they were attacking me. I was seeking validation, and any disagreement would appear to be the opposite. I focused on my negative assumption.

This is where "you reap what you sow" comes in. Negative breeds negative. Just as positive breeds positive. Both are spirals. One builds a good mood. The other tears it down. Even if you aren't aware of it, being negative tears down your well-being.

Have you felt like you can't move forward? Do you dwell on the bad and feel nothing good happens to you? You are a victim of bad luck! Then you feel bad, your mind finds more to think of as bad, and you dwell on that, and here comes the spiral downward. It is hard to see solutions when you are caught in this cycle. You begin to feel trapped, unable to find a way out. You are essentially saying that you cannot do anything about it. As a victim, you give away your power to move beyond the situation. You can become hopeless, frustrated, and stuck.

It becomes easy to blame someone else for your situation.

The trick is learning to be aware of what you are thinking and to realize that your focus is your choice. The outcome in situations often depends on what you choose to focus on.

A happy heart does good for the soul. *"A cheerful look brings joy to the heart, and good news gives health to the bones"* Proverbs 15:30. You can experience that joy as you focus on building a healthier life. Choose to release the whining and to go forward with a positive attitude. You can whine or shine! Your choice.

Start taking responsibility for your life. Take your power back. It is up to you to choose how you accept and respond to situations. Use your positive energy to build more positive energy. You've got that power within you right now!

Pick up your mirror. What do you see? Beautiful eyes? Nice hair? An inviting smile? A person who is ready to build a positive, grateful life?

Feel all that positive energy lifting you up. Feed it with happy thoughts and keep that upward spiral. Hop on over to the mirror, smile, and say, I am a positive person right now! And I like myself right now because _____, I love my life right now because _____.

DAY 3: POSITIVE ENERGY

Check the box when you are done:

☐ I like myself (3x)

☐ I love my life (3x)

Go and enjoy right now! Keep that happy-thought going. Now can you feel the positive energy? I like myself right now because... Have you added a beat? Don't forget to celebrate!

Day 4:
Self-Talk

I once saw myself and my life in a cracked mirror. I let that faulty thinking deceive me into believing everything, and everyone was against me. When I had trouble loosening a light bulb, opening a bag of grain, or fixing broken equipment, it was all about karma, the universe, fate, or whatever you wanted to call it, being against me.

Wow. I was helpless and would always be a loser. So wrong! I wasn't a loser. I gave up before I completed what I was doing. That's it. I was a quitter. I told myself I was meant to fail, and there wasn't anything I could do about it. So, I quit trying. And I told myself just how useless and incapable I was.

How do you talk to yourself? Are you encouraging? Comforting? Or do you beat yourself up until you cannot see the difference between reality and lies? If you say something or hear something enough times, you will believe it. Have you talked yourself into believing lies about yourself? You know you aren't worthless. You learned that on Day 1.

DAY 4: SELF-TALK

Maybe no one stood over you saying terrible things (perhaps they did). But you heard it through their actions of neglect, lack of respect, or rejections. Did you begin affirming these images that were said or implied by others? Have you heard yourself saying similar things?

How you talk to yourself does matter. You will believe what you say. So, you might as well say something encouraging.

Self-talk leads to self-image. Self-image is your foundation for building confidence, self-respect, and self-esteem. You can talk yourself into being a strong, empowered woman right now.

Deceitful thinking caused me a lot of pain: God was my comforter. Deceit built walls: God set me free. Lies blinded me to the truth: God opened my eyes to the truth. I saw only negativity in all things: God gave me hope.

"Teach me your way, O Lord, and I will walk in your truth" (Psalm 86:11). I gave up my attitude and opened my eyes to God's word. The truth became clear: I am a valuable child of God.

You can go forward with an attitude of thankfulness. You can look in the mirror and tell your new best friend how awesome she is! Take that negative name you used to call yourself (stupid, dumb, ugly, fat, etc.) and replace it with the opposite, positive name (smart, intelligent, beautiful, shapely, etc.). Teach her to say, I am (use your new name) and I like myself right now because _____, I love my life right now because _____.

Check the box when you are done:

- ☐ I like myself (3x)
- ☐ I love my life (3x)

Go and enjoy right now! Repeat your new name for yourself over and over.

I like myself right now because... I love my life right now because...Don't forget to celebrate!

Day 5:

Overwhelmed

How do you fill your days? Do you plan out your activities carefully? Or are you like me and have a list of everything you would like to get done in the next year on your plate for today? Not only do you identify too many things, you expect perfection from all of them. How's that working out?

Maybe you plan your day realistically, but then the kids need a ride somewhere, your husband is bringing his boss for dinner, or your aging parents are having trouble remembering daily chores. Suddenly, your plans have been buried beneath important issues.

Your situation may be different. No matter what, everyone experiences the stress of feeling overwhelmed at times.

Maybe your stress is brought on by external forces, such as your young children, your husband, or your aging parents. You do your best to meet their needs. But what about the internal stress that builds up due to your mental process of the situation? Does your mind play out every negative scenario until you feel overwhelmed and maybe even helpless? Have you repeat-

DAY 5: OVERWHELMED

ed every issue until all you have is a chaotic mess of too much information?

What expectations do others or even yourself place on you? You do have responsibilities. Do they add up to more than you think you can handle? Are you allowing your thoughts to focus on all of it at once? Your world can feel like it is caving in on you. Instead of attacking the whole list of things to do, address one issue at a time.

Sit down with pen and paper and begin to write. You may not be a writer, but you need to take your chaotic thoughts out of your head and put them on paper. Just write whatever comes to mind that you have on your to-do list. After you identify all your worries on paper, begin organizing them by priority. Maybe you are out of milk, but you can put off shopping until tomorrow. Missing milk and cereal for one day will not hurt anyone.

Beside each statement, write whether it is urgent, important, necessary but can wait, or a want, not a need. Put everything aside except the urgent. Hopefully, there aren't many of those. What has to be done now, and what can wait a while? Can any of it be done by asking for help from someone? If you can reasonably pass it off to a trusted person, do it.

When you have made a workable plan for the first urgent issue, take a break. Laugh, smile, breathe. Relax and then tackle the next urgent issue, then the next—one at a time.

Some stress can be beneficial. It can motivate you to do something. However, when it becomes a barrier, you need to take it apart and examine one piece at a time. I have always had the habit of listing things I had to do, then looking around to see how much more I could add. You know, I have to pay the bills, take kids to ballgames, find the accounting errors on the taxes, fix my husband's lunch...so I might as well add in the laundry, dishes, visiting a sick friend, and anything else I could be doing. Do you pile it all on and then wonder why you feel overwhelmed?

Decipher each issue. Make a reasonable plan with each one. Don't pretend you are some kind of super-woman. You are just one person. A fantastic person, but only one person. You must take care of yourself to avoid being overwhelmed. Then you can continue being that amazing person.

Look in the mirror and remind yourself that you are worth it.

TAKING CARE OF YOURSELF IS NOT A LUXURY. IT IS A NECESSITY.

Look in the mirror and say, I am an amazing person, and I like myself right now because _____, I love my life right now because _____.

Check the box when you are done:

☐ I like myself (3x)

☐ I love my life (3x)

You can face your challenges because you like yourself and you love your life! Take care of yourself right now. And celebrate who you are becoming!

Day 6:

Labels

I remember an incident that a couple experienced when they arrived in our town after leaving their country following the Vietnam war. The couple, who did not speak or read any English, went to the grocery store to find something to eat with the small amount of money they had. They searched the aisles for what was available without preparation but within their budget. Finally, they settled on a container with a picture of crisp pieces of chicken. They hurried home and opened up what they thought would be their dinner. Shock and surprise overtook them when they peeled back the top and discovered a solid, white oily substance. Inside the container, there were no pieces of fried chicken. The Crisco label had misled them.

Are you carrying labels that are not accurate for who you really are? Have you accepted the labels that others may have stuck on you? They are a heavy weight to carry and can crush your spirit of hope. Peel off all those false tags. If you have been carrying them awhile, it may not be easy. But, it is essential.

I grew up feeling I was overweight and unattractive. I was familiar with being called many things that were

DAY 6: LABELS

not flattering. Each time I heard them, I hurt deep inside. That did not stop me from accepting the label and attaching it to the image of myself.

Like I said before, when you repeat something often enough, even if it is a lie, you begin to believe it. I had no reason not to believe that I was fat, ugly, and worthless, so I accepted those as accurate descriptions. My beliefs about myself--what I could do and how people reacted to me--all came from the false beliefs that were laid as my foundation. I said I was worthless, so I felt worthless. That drove my belief that I could not do anything right, confirming my worthlessness and pounding home the lie.

How you talk to yourself and how you see yourself make a big difference in moving toward your goal. Yank those labels off. It actually feels good. Free yourself to find new, positive labels. Replace the old with labels from God.

Peeling those labels was not easy. I accepted Christ as my Savior when I was young. That didn't immediately change my foundation. Others still used the old labels. When I graduated high school, I attended a one-year Bible school. I learned so much about the Bible. But I still did not wash the old labels off. I left the college and went into the world carrying Bible knowledge and the old image of myself. The future was disastrous.

I knew what God said, but I still looked to man for acceptance and validation of my value. I would say that man failed me, but it was my expectation of man that failed. Your validation for your life does not come from man. I wasted years waiting for someone to come along and fix the distorted thinking that kept me in depression.

I did not open my eyes to the truth until after I attempted to take my life. Did I really want to die? No. What I really wanted was to enjoy life. I wanted to feel like I was okay, not full of flaws. I wanted to find a better way to live than I had been living.

When I was in the hospital, I didn't like how I was treated. When I was in the waiting room at the mental health clinic, I didn't want to be "one of them." Well, then I had to stop acting like "one of them" and find a different way to look at my life.

I had been waiting around for someone to find me, see my problem, and fix me. No, that knight in shining armor wasn't showing up. The only person who could fix me was me. I had to take responsibility for how I saw myself and tear off all those old labels from the past. Are you waiting for someone to fix you? It is you who has to make the decision to change, but you don't have to do it alone.

I stopped waiting for someone to rescue me from false beliefs. I began pretending I was okay when I was around people. When I was no longer moody and sad, trying to be a wallflower, people began to treat me differently. I was starting to feel accepted. I had searched for validation from people while I was pushing them away with my moods and attitudes. I was a slave to misguided thinking.

The other thing, and the most important, was that I began seeing who God said I was. *"You are no longer a slave, but a son; and since you are a son, God has made you also an heir"* (Galatians 4:7).

DAY 6: LABELS

I began attending church and joined a women's study group. The subject, Fulfilled Womanhood, was about being a Godly wife and mother. I never planned on being either, but to keep from being alone all weekend, I went. It became one of the most significant turning points in my life.

In describing a Godly mother, the subject hit me hard. This was not a description of my mother. Suddenly, God showed me that my life problems were not my fault. I was raised with false beliefs. How did I come to accept all those lies? Because it was all I knew.

I may have felt worthless way back then, but today I feel priceless because I am a child of God. That label, I accept and claim every day. You can look in the mirror and claim it also.

On Day 4, you chose a new, positive name to call yourself. Write it on your mirror. Every time you see it, smile and say, "Yes, that is me!" Then celebrate! I like myself right now because _____, I love my life right now because _____.

Check the box when you are done:

☐ I like myself (3x)

☐ I love my life (3x)

Celebrate your new, positive label! Can you feel that internal happy-dance building?

Day 7:
Expectations

Have you ever waited for someone to do something and was then disappointed in their action? They did not respond the way you expected. You were let down. But was it the person who let you down or your own expectations?

I waited years, expecting my knight in shining armor to ride in and rescue me from my lack of self-esteem. He never showed up. Instead of being responsible for my own happiness, I was relying on someone else. I knew I saw no value in myself, and I waited for someone to tell me otherwise.

So many times, I tore myself apart and waited for someone to coddle me. I wanted soft, encouraging words to sway me into seeing something positive about myself. I expected someone else to find the good in me. Usually, it was just pointed out that I had self-esteem issues. Well, no duh! I knew that. I just didn't know how to change it.

I went to counselors expecting to have them spell out exactly what I needed to do. I wasn't always happy with the results. At times there were little nuggets of

DAY 7: EXPECTATIONS

truth that I could pick out and apply. When asked about going to college, my reply was, "Do you know how old I will be when I get out?" Her answer was, "And how old will you be in four years if you don't go to college?"

That was an eye-opener. I was expecting good things to happen right now. In reality, I had to work for it. I began seeing how my distorted thinking was actually lies.

It is healthy to have high expectations and build hope. But what do you do while anticipating your desired results?

Your expectations are just that; your expectations. They don't suddenly materialize without some planning or action on your part.

I was relying on other people to make me happy. Did I try to see myself differently? Or act friendly around people others? No, I sat and waited for that magic wand to sprinkle fairy dust over me and make my life wonderful. Well, maybe that's not entirely accurate, but I did not work at building a better life. I had to hit bottom before I began encouraging myself to think positive.

Do you set yourself up for failure but having unrealistic expectations? You know, like planning to do more in one day than humanly possible and then beating yourself up. You don't have to shoot for the moon every day. Be realistic.

First, know yourself. I never really knew myself because I was focused on pleasing others. Bad idea! Get to know yourself. What do you like? Not like? What are your capabilities? Pat yourself on the back when you experience even small successes. Dream big! Set your goals high! But don't overwhelm yourself by trying to do too much at once, and don't set yourself up to fail by doing nothing.

Expectations should encourage you to strive, not weigh you down.

Pick up your mirror. Look at the person looking back and say, "I am only one person. I have to take care of myself to get anything done. Therefore, I will not try to do everything."

When you look in the mirror, what do you expect to see? A photoshopped model? Or a valuable child of God? Stop looking for the flaws and see what God sees. Don't forget the new name you are calling yourself. Is it written on your mirror, so you don't forget? Celebrate you, just the way you are. You may need a bigger celebration gesture to keep up with your growth? Try adding a little movement of the hips while you go to the mirror and say, "Hello, (use your new name)! I like myself right now because _____, I love my life right now because _____.

Check the box when you are done:

☐ I like myself (3x)

☐ I love my life (3x)

Go and enjoy right now. Keep celebrating that you are awesome!

Day 8:

Your Past

Hold the mirror up. What do you see, besides your beautiful face? What is behind you? How many times do you try to move forward while dragging everything that is behind you?

Yes, your past shaped and molded you. It is what formed you today. However, how are you dealing with the things that happened to you?

Remember how you buried your value? To dig that valuable treasure up, you may need to dig up some of your past.

Digging up the past is not meant to allow you to point fingers or assign blame. Everyone has their own problems. The person or persons who hurt you are most likely not people who are at peace with themselves.

The most common abusers are people who we know and often trust, such as parents. Kids don't come with an instruction manual, and if your parents weren't raised in constructive homes, then the task of parenting was even more challenging. Parents make errors. However, your parents' mistakes don't have to define your life, no matter how demeaning they were. The damage is

DAY 8: YOUR PAST

done, and scars remain, but understanding the origin of your faulty thinking is the beginning of healing.

Maybe someone took advantage of you. You don't have to be an abused woman. You are a woman who was abused. Someone was at fault, and you were helpless. If you are in that position now, get out. Please find help with a trusted friend, organization, or police agency. Find a safe way to leave that life behind. No one can do it for you. If you want change, which you deserve, then you have to be the one to take that first step. There will be others to help you along the way. See resources in the back of this book for more ideas.

Okay. Back to preventing your past experiences from tripping up your future plans.

Whether your pain was from childhood or it came later in life, it is not your place to seek revenge or entertain pity. Whoever hurt you will be accountable before God, who has seen it all. *"Nothing in all creation is hidden from God's sight. Everything is uncovered and laid bare before the eyes of the Creator to whom we must give account"* (Hebrews 4:13).

You may have been abused, betrayed, neglected, rejected, or many horrible things. However, your Savior has experienced it also. You can seek understanding and empathy from someone who knows what it is like to be in your darkness and pain. Knowing Jesus has your back, you can lay your past to rest.

When I was growing up, I believed everything that happened to me was my fault. That distorted thought remained as I went through life, and I saw many situations with a twisted view. I carried the blame, embarrassment and was full of grief as I trudged on. If I realized that someone else could be in the wrong, I would have been relieved. Instead of calling myself names, my thinking would have been more like, "Boy, that guy was a jerk. I didn't deserve that remark." Or, "I am not an idiot. I just didn't see what he saw." That is the type of self-talk that can help.

That mess of stuff from your past doesn't define you unless you want it to. If your reactions today mirror the pain of yesterday, you need to take a closer look at it and see why you are hanging on. Ask yourself if you are reacting reasonably to something uncomfortable. Or is your reaction off the chart for the present situation? If so, it may really be connected to the past.

Look at those who injured you. Have you forgiven them? Yes, I said forgive them. We will discuss that tomorrow.

Is the image in the mirror looking to a great future, or is it staring at what is behind you? The focus really matters. Look yourself in the eye and say, "My past doesn't define me. I am who I choose to be!" Now that deserves a really big celebration!

Grab your mirror and put a tune to:

I like myself right now because _____ and I love my life right now because _____.

Check the box when you are done:

☐ I like myself (3x)

☐ I love my life (3x)

Go and enjoy right now! Celebrate your fresh start!

Day 9:

Forgiveness

We said we were going to talk about forgiveness today. Does just thinking about forgiving a particular person make your blood boil? Then we need to talk.

Have you ever been told you need to forgive someone, and your response was, "But....?"

The Bible says there are no exceptions. *"Be kind and compassionate to one another, forgiving each other, just as in Christ God forgave you"* (Ephesians 4:32).

Imagine you are a caterpillar. You just gorged yourself on everything you could eat, which we have all done, and you sleep comfortably in your cocoon while transformation occurs. You wake up a beautiful butterfly and are eager to fly. After all, that is what you have been waiting for your whole life. You wave your wings until they are strong and attempt to lift yourself into the air. Only you haven't shed the hard cast that encompassed you while you were changing. You can't pull yourself up and fly freely.

That is what you are doing with unforgiveness if you are holding on to anger, bitterness, and revenge. You

DAY 9: FORGIVENESS

may be seeking a new life, but until you get rid of all the trappings of unforgiveness, you aren't going far.

"For if you forgive men when they sin against you, your heavenly Father will also forgive you. But if you do not forgive men their sins, you Father will not forgive your sins." (Matthew 6:14-15). There are no exceptions. It is pretty clear.

I will grant you it isn't easy to forgive someone who harmed you, especially when they don't care about your pain. But the scripture is talking to you. The act of forgiving is an act of obedience. If you don't obey, nothing happens to the one you are holding a grudge against. If you don't forgive, you are the one eaten away by bitterness and vindictiveness. The command to forgive is for your good. Like the butterfly carrying his casting, you can't be what you were intended to be when you are infested with unforgiveness.

Yes, infested. It will grow and multiply if you aren't willing to clean it out.

Think of it another way: have you ever sinned? Any type of sin? Sin is "missing the mark" that God has established. Hitting the mark is beyond human capacity. Therefore we all have sinned. Did Jesus forgive you? Did you deserve it? Were you glad that He had the grace and love to forgive you?

Who do you need to forgive? If your heartbeat quickens when a particular person's name is mentioned, you have unforgiven issues. Ask God to show you who you need to release from your anger. How do you do that? You start by asking God to give you His love for the person. You may not be able to love, but God loves them the same as He loves you. Talk to God about the person. Don't ask God to inflict your judgment, but ask God to speak to their heart. Pray that you would come to see them through Christ's eyes. Be concerned about their salvation. You are not freeing them from responsibility. You are freeing yourself from bitterness that destroys your ability to honor God.

How far do you think the butterfly makes it with the dry, worthless casting still attached to him? Are you ready to shed the confining bondage of unforgiveness and allow fresh hope to strengthen your faith? Free yourself to become what you have been waiting your whole life to become.

Go to your mirror and say, I like myself right now because _____. I love my life right now because _____.

Check the box when you are done:

☐ I like myself (3x)

☐ I love my life (3x)

Go and enjoy right now! Celebrate your freedom to grow and become all you can be!

Day 10:

Distorted Thoughts

Have you ever had a conversation with yourself that went something like this: "I know they aren't going to listen to me? They never do. They will say my idea won't work. Why do I bother?"

Your conversation may vary, but I bet it has the same kind of distortions. First, are you a fortune-teller? How do you know what will happen? The probability may be high, but you can't know for sure. And have they never listened to you, or does it just seem that way? Words like never and always are signs of exaggeration. Again, you can't know what they will say.

So, let's take your last sentence, "Why do I bother?" You bother because you care. You did your best because it matters to you. Don't tear it down before you even present it.

Can I tell you a story? Actually, it is kind of embarrassing, but it demonstrates how distorted conversations with yourself can work.

When I was in college, two of my friends worked and were always late for our noon class. I said I would help them out by fixing lunch for them to eat during

DAY 10: DISTORTED THOUGHTS

class. One day, as I grilled their cheese sandwiches, I was distracted, and they got a little dark. OK, they had some burnt along one side. I didn't have time to remake them, so I wrapped them up and headed to class. All the way, I kept telling myself how dumb I was to let them burn, how the guys will say something about the condition of their lunch, how I never get anything right, and so on. You know the "pep" talk. I felt terrible by the time I got to class. I took the negative spiral even further. I reminded myself what a jerk I was, how everyone laughed at my failings, no one ever appreciated that I tried. I was nearly in tears with all the tearing apart of myself. Then the guys came rushing into class and sat next to me. I tossed their sandwiches to them and waited for their comments. Sure enough, the first one pointed out the dark side of the bread.

My dark side blew up. I grabbed the sandwich and proceeded to pound it to the thickness of a piece of paper (ok, that may be an exaggeration). The guys stared, wide-eyed. The class turned to look. And I sat, jaws clenched, looking straight ahead.

Do you see how distorted thinking works? I talked myself into being upset without any real foundation. I wasn't dumb for getting the bread too dark. Yes, I knew the guys would comment on their sandwiches. I could have said, "Take it or leave it." But my reaction was over-the-top. No one expected or deserved my crazy response.

Cognitive distortions are habitual ways of thinking that are often inaccurate and negatively based. "I will never learn to drive." Or, "Nothing ever works." Are examples of statements that are commonly used but usually inaccurate. "If I try, I may learn to drive" is closer to the truth. "This time, it didn't work" is better. Everyone has used some distorted thinking from time to time.

Have you ever untangled a cord of Christmas lights that have been wadded up? It takes a lot of work, and just when you think you are winning the battle, it can form another snag. Untangling your distorted thoughts could be just as hard. In the opening scenario, you "know" they won't like your idea. Are you preparing yourself for disappointment and setting yourself up for failure? You tell yourself how no one will like your idea, so what happens when someone has a question concerning it? Do you react like I did with the sandwiches and set others up for a defensive battle?

If you had told yourself that your idea was built on a solid foundation and presented it with the confidence that it was the greatest idea ever, you might not be defensive but eager to share more details.

Awareness of what you are thinking is the first step in correcting any behavior. Train yourself to hear your statements and ask if they are negative, unreal, or over-generalizing. Reframe those thoughts right away. Don't let them begin that spiral downward. Take control. Replace them with positive, happy thoughts. Do you think I would have smashed the sandwiches if I had praised myself for helping out friends with a not-so-perfect, yet edible, lunch?

Untangle your string of thoughts and let your conversations shine brighter. Celebrate your new habit of energizing positive speaking. Celebrate with a little more energy.

DAY 10: DISTORTED THOUGHTS

Grab your mirror, smile and say, I like myself right now because _____. I love my life right now because _____.

Check the box when you are done:

☐ I like myself (3x)

☐ I love my life (3x)

Go and enjoy right now! You are growing! Celebrate!

Day 11:

Victim Mindset

"One day, my ship will come in, and with my luck, I'll probably be at the airport." Charlie Brown, as part of Snoopisms by Marie Olsen. Charlie Brown is the proud owner of Snoopy in Charles M. Schulz's cartoons. He is known for his bad luck, especially in baseball.

Like many of us, Charlie Brown has an attitude problem. He thinks bad luck is his companion, and there isn't anything he can do about it. He has a victim mentality. He feels life is happening to him, and he has no control.

We talked yesterday about exaggerating your problems or situations by using always, never, or like words. Anything bad happens, and you act like it is the end of the world. You feel powerless and begin telling yourself negative distortions about yourself.

This is another faulty thinking pattern in which you believe you are a victim when things don't go as planned. You may feel the world is out to get you. Let's look closer. Are you really hopeless?

DAY 11: VICTIM MINDSET

A victim mindset is based on a strong belief that everything is against you. Maybe you never had enough when growing up, and you feel that everything in life is a struggle. Do you think that success and happiness are for "them" and not you? You resort to thinking that you were destined to be the negative image you have of yourself. Not true! You have choices.

You need to think bigger. Remember, you got rid of the distorted thinking yesterday. Norman Vincent Peale said, "Change your thoughts and you change your world." So, let's change your world.

Look around you. Are you surrounded by people you want to be like? Are you learning from them by watching how they act and speak? You are, whether you realize it or not. If the people you bring into your life are not the ones you look up to, you need to rethink your friendships. Have you ever heard the saying, "birds of a feather flock together?" Well, it is true. You need to flock to the ones you want to be like.

You may have to start small. Hang out with people at the gym, library, or church. Take note of their actions. Do they act like every mistake is the end of the world? Do they blame others? Probably not. Are they grateful for what they have and give out compliments freely? Do they claim to be victims, or do they dream big and work toward their goals?

Being consciously aware that you need to change how you think is the best starting point. Also, surround yourself with people who have already made it or at least are actively working toward improving their lives. Remove things or even people who are holding you back.

You can plan big goals and believe that you can achieve them. You are what you believe, so believe in yourself.

Don't wait for your opportunities to come to you. Follow Jonathan Winters' advice, "If your ship doesn't come in, swim out to meet it." Be proactive in charting your future.

Pick up your mirror. You know the routine. Take your celebration stance and find your rhythm: "I like myself right now because _____. I love my life right now because _____.

Check the box when you are done:

☐ I like myself (3x)

☐ I love my life (3x)

Go and enjoy right now! Celebrate today!

Day 12:
Triggers

Do you have allergies that cause severe sneezing or coughing? Have you found out what causes your reaction? To avoid those uncomfortable feelings associated with allergies, do you look for and stay away from the items which you are allergic to? Most people do. But what about those things that you react to emotionally?

You know, that uncle that always upsets you with his array of noises while eating. That coworker who rubs you the wrong way with his snide remarks. Maybe it is not the person, but the way they said something. You detect you were attacked by their tone. You have a feeling of being there before, and the situation takes you back there again. You react as if you are reliving that memory. Well, you are. Trigger points can take you to unwanted places and stir up all the emotions that go with them.

Have you ever had a reaction that seemed far too excessive for the situation? You may have responded to a trigger that tripped up your logical reasoning of what was happening. Maybe the circumstance was going along normally, then someone said something in

DAY 12: TRIGGERS

the wrong tone, and you attacked their words or even their motives. Everyone steps back, "Wow, where did that come from?"

You may know, you may not. Somewhere in your past, an incident involved whose words or tones. The reminder may have taken you briefly out of the present and into a place where things didn't end so well for you. Survival mode kicks in, and you respond.

Triggers such as a memory, a physical sensation, or an emotion may take you back to a similar setting that was an impactful moment in your life. Your body goes right along with your mind's deception and begins to sweat. Your pulse goes up, and your breathing becomes rapid. You may even feel the tension in your jaws or gut or smell and feel the surroundings.

In flash-back mode, specific thought patterns or influences may override the current situation and create a false setting. An inner voice may be changing real to imaginary messages. What your brain interpreted was not what was happening. In the wrong setting, this can have a negative ending.

Maybe your reactions don't set off such dramatic scenes. They can be simple reactions of anger or defensiveness. They can produce any reaction that goes beyond what may be expected for the situation. The best way to handle this is to get out in front of it before it gets out of control.

First, recognize your physical warning ahead of reactions. Do you feel tension in your gut or an increase in your heart rate and breathing? Is that little inner voice getting louder, "He meant..." At this point, you need to step back, at least mentally, and ask yourself,

"Am I sure that was his intention?" Don't let your assumptions run wild.

Second, pinpoint the cause. Take a breath and consider what the trigger was and where it came from. Were there certain words that someone used against you at one time? Was it the attitude that made you feel belittled or rejected? Think for a minute. Was the present reaction a misinterpretation?

Then, make a decision about how you want to feel at that moment.

Finally, take responsibility for your reaction and actively change your emotional state. To relax during the episode, practice some humming to distract you.

Whew, you made it through that episode. Make a plan so the next time will be easier. If you recognize certain situations that may set off triggers, you can protect yourself by avoiding them. If at all possible, keep yourself out of situations where there is a chance a trigger may be set off. If you know that loud noises remind you of gunfire, stay away from the fireworks. If dark places set up your defenses, remain in the light.

If you can't avoid a hotspot, plan to be silent. Don't respond to remarks or body language. Look the other way. Use the relaxation tools you learned.

Look ahead. If there are potential trouble areas, prepare a strategy for handling them. Don't rely on stopping a reaction once it has been set off.

It may take work, but it is worth it to take control of your unruly emotions.

DAY 12: TRIGGERS

Pick up your mirror and say, "I have taken control of my triggers! And, I like myself right now because _____, I love my life right now because _____."

Check the box when you are done:

☐ I like myself (3x)

☐ I love my life (3x)

Go and enjoy right now! Celebrate your new control over your emotions.

Day 13:

Boundaries

Have you ever felt someone took advantage of you? Did they ask too much of you? And they never gave back?

Growing up, I didn't have much guidance. I swayed in whichever direction I felt would get me in less trouble at home. It was pretty shaky footing.

After high school, I didn't have any definite goals for my future. I went to a Bible College for one year and then moved to where my friends were going to school. No plans. Just hanging out with them. My future was in jeopardy. First, I had no foundation, and second, I had no goals: nothing to stand on and nothing to reach for.

I didn't have a long-term plan or a sense of value, so I was soon deep in depression and anxiety. I was waiting for someone to see that I had a problem and fix me. That knight in shining armor on a valiant white stallion wasn't showing up. Who showed up was an older man who was an elder in the church I attended. He said he counseled many people and knew I had social and emotional issues, and would be willing to counsel me. I thought my prayers were answered. But when he showed up at my apartment late one night when my roommate was gone, I felt very uncomfortable.

He began describing how women should always fall under the protection of a man. Since I was single, I needed that attachment. He talked about submission and enjoying physical intimacy, and I had to learn that before I could really be happy. I knew this was way off base. I tried to get up from the couch, but he ran his hand up my leg then across my chest to hold me under his control. Tears filled my eyes, and I felt sick. Finally, I was able to push him away and told him to leave.

I never told anyone what happened that night. How could I? It was my fault for being so stupid. A normal person would have seen it coming. I left the church, and he remained an elder.

Were you raised to set limits on what was acceptable and what wasn't? Or were you encouraged to not step on toes? Was it better to let others make you feel uncomfortable than to voice that discomfort? Do you focus on someone else's needs instead of your own? You may be afraid to create tension in a relationship, or you may be seeking just to be liked. However, you then accept other people's limits or lack thereof. In doing so, you can lose your own identity.

I didn't know what boundaries were or how to set them. I would agree with people just to feel that I was liked. My needs and values were ignored.

Setting boundaries are essential to your mental health, self-respect, and having healthy relationships. If you haven't established boundaries and let people know what your expectations are, they probably don't know. Most people aren't mind readers, and unless you tell them, they may not realize they have crossed a line. Having boundaries protects you. In other words, you are teaching people how to treat you.

A healthy relationship has a give and take to it. When you become a people-pleaser, that is lost. When you never learn to separate the needs of others from your own, you can fail to know your own needs. The desire to be liked is a normal human need. But when that desire supersedes self-protection, it is unhealthy.

Have you ever engaged in self-destructive behavior to feel you belonged? You may have had a history of being mistreated and seek to improve that by pleasing others. But without limits, those actions are dangerous and can become a way of life.

Do you feel burdened by doing what you think others want? Do you avoid speaking up until you are ready to explode? You are not responsible for others. You are responsible for taking care of yourself. *"Each of us will give account of himself to God"* (Romans 14:2).

Instead of ignoring your needs, the other side of not having boundaries is only thinking of your needs and ignoring everyone else's. You know that person and their sense of entitlement. Setting limits also guides you on how to treat other people and honor their limits.

Give yourself permission to set boundaries. Be assertive in keeping those boundaries in place. Solid boundaries prevent you from making spur-of-the-moment decisions. Celebrate your healthy boundaries and the freedom that will give you in making choices. You go, Girl!

DAY 13: BOUNDARIES

Hop on over to your mirror, get in the beat, and sing, "I like myself right now because _____, I love my life right now because _____.

Check the box when you are done:

☐ I like myself (3x)

☐ I love my life (3x)

Go and enjoy right now! Don't forget to celebrate your control with boundaries.

Day 14:
Today's Decisions, Tomorrow's Dreams

Making decisions is something you do every day. It means there is a fork in the road. The answer could be either this way or that way. You choose. Your future depends on it.

How do you usually make those choices? Toss a coin? Close your eyes and point? Those are not very trustworthy. Making decisions has always been difficult for me. I used to worry about what others wanted to hear or if they would criticize my answer. Even simple things like, "what is your favorite color?" At times, my answers would be vague so that I could adjust them if needed. I never thought about what I liked.

It is just as unhealthy to avoid making a decision as it is to make the wrong decision. I had no plan, goal, or dream for my life, nor did I know who I was and what I wanted. That left me vulnerable to the whims of others who didn't have my best in mind.

Do you have a goal that you are working for? Have you planned your route to that goal? How do you know

DAY 14: TODAY'S DECISIONS, TOMORROW'S DREAMS

which road to take unless you know where you are going? Don't let others determine your future.

Decisions you make today will either take you toward your goal or present a block or detour to it. Maybe you want to go to college and have saved some money, but that money could buy a new TV and entertainment center. You rationalize that the entertainment center would be for your family. You would be selfish to keep the funds for yourself. Sounds logical, doesn't it? You are not going to reach your goal with that compromise. You need to hold firmly to the path, or you won't make it. Which is more important? The TV or the career? Short-term gratification or long-term goal-building?

If you always have short-term thinking, how are you going to gain your long-term benefits? You need to stick to your plan, or you will drift with what looks good at the moment. Are you honestly working toward your goal every day, or are you setting yourself up to fail? Maybe deep down, you don't feel you deserve your goal. Are you sabotaging yourself?

What you do today will always affect where you are tomorrow.

Making decisions can be stressful, especially if you don't have the confidence to make mistakes. You can let your mind churn with too many options, or you can sort them out.

When I was 48 years old, my life took a big turn. I had a good life that I was happy with. Then I lost my health. I went from being very active outdoors, riding my horse, working on the farm, spending time with friends, to being nearly bed-ridden. I spent the next two years traveling to nineteen different doctors in two states. I had tough decisions to make.

I found comfort in, *""For I know the plans I have for you," declares the Lord, "plans to prosper you and not to harm you, plans to give you hope and a future""* (Jeremiah 29:11).

The parts that spoke to me were *"not to harm you,"* which gave me hope in struggling with my physical condition, and *"a future,"* God had a plan even if I didn't know what it was. I could celebrate His promise. You can too. Celebrate that you can decide today to stay on the path for a great tomorrow.

Time now to grab your mirror and sing, "I like myself right now because _____, I love my life right now because _____.

Check the box when you are done:

☐ I like myself (3x)

☐ I love my life (3x)

Go and enjoy right now! Do today what creates a great tomorrow. Celebrate your choices.

Day 15:

Comparing

Have you ever compared an apple and a banana? What are you actually comparing? That makes as much sense as comparing yourself with other people, which we all do. Even when it doesn't make you better, smarter, or happier. What's the benefit?

That depends.

Comparing yourself with a peer can be normal and even essential if you use the information to set a benchmark for yourself. You have a fundamental need to evaluate yourself, and you do that by using others as a reference. Self-reflection helps you define your character, and that can be refined in relationship with others. You see where you fit in and establish ways to improve. Is the result encouraging you?

Or is comparing yourself to someone else causing you to tear down the other person? When you compare to see yourself more favorably and boost your self-esteem, you tend to minimize the other person's favorable aspects. You find fault with them in an attempt to feel better about yourself.

DAY 15: COMPARING

Usually, the person you are comparing yourself to is someone similar to you in some way that you think is important. If you are a runner, you will compare yourself to a local champion instead of an Olympic athlete.

Let's do some comparing. Imagine you have two pieces of the same fruit. Remember, they have to be similar on the outside. Place one on the counter a couple feet away from you. Hold the other. First, what can you see in the fruit on the counter? Is it deep-colored and flawless? What else can you know about it? You can't pick it up—no walking around it. Just look at it from where you are. Besides its color, size, and shape, what do you really know?

Look at the fruit in your hand. Examine it all the way around. Squeeze it just a little. Rub your hand over it. Smell it. Did you notice the dark spot on the backside? Was it firm or soft? Smooth and round? Or did it have bumps on it? Do you know more about this fruit than the one on the counter? Wait, don't stop examining it.

Peel the fruit in your hand. Does it still smell the same? What about the sections? Are they uniform and moist? Are some of the sections dry? Does it have seeds?

We could go on. Which one do you know more about? Which one can you establish an opinion about? Pretty simple.

So how is it fair – or even helpful – to compare yourself, who you know thoroughly inside and out, to someone you are looking at from a distance. Remember how you were holding the mirror close to your face? You saw every flaw, which the other person can't see when they are standing farther away.

Comparing yourself in an attempt to boost your self-esteem will make you miserable because you are not comparing equal pictures. It may make you feel inferior or superior, temporarily. But when you dwell on it, do you feel angry, resentful, or toxic?

You have a pre-existing self-concept. If that view is positive, then healthy comparisons can help you grow and improve. However, if your self-concept is lacking, your comparisons can be challenging. You are comparing to confirm what you already believe, which may be distorted. You will keep your world consistent with your view of yourself.

To make your comparisons healthy, establish a healthy self-view before you get started. Make sure you are your own best friend and take care of yourself. Write down achievements that you are proud of to remind yourself when your inner voice says that you are less-than someone else. Even if it is a small win such as "I made it through the day without crying." Read through your achievements every day, so you don't forget what you are capable of.

The distorted realities on social media can also pull you down. People tend to make themselves look better. Don't let their posts cause you distress. They may not even be true.

You will never run out of things to compare. Remember, you are your own worst critic and yet compare that with the best of others. Set a reasonable benchmark for yourself. Practice healthy comparisons and create a clearer focus on who you are, giving you the energy to enjoy time with others. Celebrate the fact that you are unique.

DAY 15: COMPARING

Pick up your mirror. By now, you know what is coming. Say, "I like myself right now because _____, and I love my life right now because _____.

Check the box when you are done:

☐ I like myself (3x)

☐ I love my life (3x)

Go and celebrate right now! Sing to yourself, "I like myself right now because.....!

Day 16:

Competition

Competition is rampant within society. There are physical teams, intellectual teams, and teams for just about everything. There is a lot of money in the playing of competitive games. If not a participant, many people become obsessed with watching others beat it out for the win.

But how does competition affect you? Chances are you aren't a professional, so how do you compete in your daily life?

Whether in a job, career, or school, you have the opportunity to compete in your daily life. Maybe you just want to have the nicest lawn on the block. Or drive the nicest car to work. Mothers often want to have the most well-behaved toddler in the room. (Good luck with that!)

By itself, competition is neither good nor bad. Healthy competition is a test of your physical or mental capacity, not your self-value. Challenging yourself in healthy ways can lead to feeling happy and empowered. Especially if you can enjoy the rewards of your success.

DAY 16: COMPETITION

When you work hard and win, your brain releases dopamine, a feel-good hormone that increases euphoria, bliss, and a surge of energy. And the brain wants to experience that feeling again and again.

But what happens when you don't win? Competing to build your self-esteem can lead to jealousy, stress, and exhaustion.

Do you like the feeling of winning? Or do you like the feeling of being better than someone else? You may be more skilled in a specific area, but winning doesn't make you more valuable than anyone else. Just as losing doesn't make you less valuable. It's been said that "The only person you should try to be better than is the person you were yesterday."

I used to think that every time I lost was proof that I was worthless. Mostly I blamed losing in sports on the fact that I was overweight. If I lost at table games, it was because I was stupid. I had a lot of excuses. None had anything to do with learning the game, practicing, or preparing for competition. It was just that fate thing. The universe was against me! Hogwash!

Are we born competitors? Competition has been at the core of the survival of the human species since the beginning of time. It was necessary for survival. The bravest, fastest, or most skilled found food and survived. Today it is the thrill of the sport and the glory of winning that spur participants into a struggle to outdo each other.

Do you enjoy competing to develop skills? Or is it a way to see if you "measure up?"

When we were young, my sister and I would race across the field. As soon as she would get ahead of me, I would quit. I wasn't a born competitor. I believed I was a born loser. Why fight nature? I felt someone would always beat me, so I learned to give myself the first punch. I quit and criticized myself before anyone else could. I showed them I knew where I stood: at the bottom of the pile. I would become angry at myself and pessimistic that I would never improve.

In competing, do you respect the other players or feel the need to win to boost your self-esteem? Healthy competition is respectful and cooperative.

"A flower does not think of competing with the flower next to it. It just blooms" Zen Shin. Life is not a competition.

Are you doing the best you can each day? That makes you a winner. Your value as a person is not determined by whether you win or lose when measured against someone else. Your character may be displayed when you react to winning or losing, but your value is not affected.

"But those who hope in the Lord will renew their strength. They will soar on wings like eagles; they will run and not grow weary; they will walk and not be faint" (Isaiah 40:31).

You can soar simply by knowing your self-worth.

It is time to look in the mirror and proclaim that self-worth. Do you have the rhythm down yet? "I like myself right now because _____, I love my life right now because _____."

DAY 16: COMPETITION

Check the box when you are done:

☐ I like myself (3x)

☐ I love my life (3x)

Go and enjoy right now! You are already better than you were yesterday. Celebrate!

Day 17:
Sabotaging Yourself

Pick up your mirror. Look at the image there. That is the person who may be blocking your forward progress. You can be your own worst enemy!

Remember how I said I really wanted someone to affirm that I was okay? What did I do to gain that confirmation? I pushed people away with my depressed, sad, and pessimistic attitude. I am not saying I wanted to be depressed, sad, or pessimistic, but those are things most people don't want to be around. These behaviors were fed by my negative self-talk and prevented me from reaching my goal of acceptance.

A cycle began to form: I felt inadequate and created ways to cause failures, and because of the failure, I felt inadequate. This reinforced negative behaviors that ate away at my potential and set me up for more failures, with the resulting failures and disappointments creating more feelings of guilt and frustration. Do you see the spiral downward?

My belief that I didn't deserve any better in life was holding me back. I had a conflict between what I wanted and what I projected to others. I was definitely my

DAY 17: SABOTAGING YOURSELF

own worst enemy! To enjoy life, I had to remove the sabotaging behavior.

Later, when I pretended that I was happy and began interacting with people positively, they began reacting to me differently.

Do you take responsibility for your actions, or do you blame others for failures? Do you think carefully before making decisions and consider the consequences? You may be sabotaging yourself if you are not developing a well-thought-out plan, then putting that plan into action. Are you able to say "No," when you know you don't have time for another project? Adding one more thing for you to do is a common way of sabotaging the outcome. Then you blame someone else and resort to negative self-talk.

Remember the story on Day 14 when you had to decide between the entertainment center and saving for college? If you bought the entertainment center, you were sabotaging your future education. Your own action resulted in not progressing toward your goal.

When your husband comes home after a tiring day and comments on dinner not being ready, do you react with defense and assume he is accusing you of not doing what you should? You have had a hectic day and will have dinner ready shortly. Instead of explaining in a kind voice, you snap back that he always puts you down. What follows is not pleasant, and no one is happy. You just sabotaged a peaceful evening.

Have you ever complained about someone else without going to them with your concern? You may have sabotaged the solution and the relationship by spreading information to a third (or fourth) party.

You know that cheesecake you ate last night before bed? That was you sabotaging your weight loss. Boy, am I familiar with that one! I have fought my weight all my life. My first weight-loss diet was when I was in the fourth grade. I learned to see being overweight as a character flaw. That reinforced my already low self-esteem but didn't keep me from overeating. Self-sabotage to low self-esteem, and you have that downward spiral.

There is a way out. As in most cases, the first step is recognizing behavior that is sabotaging your progress.

When you recognize what you are doing, you can begin to monitor your behaviors, feelings, and thoughts around your actions. Are you letting your emotions take over when you react? Do you stop and think of the consequences of how you proceed?

"But now you must rid yourselves of all such things as these: anger, rage, malice, slander, and filthy language from your lips" (Colossians 3:8).

Get rid of, or at least suppress your anger before you speak. Manage your emotions instead of letting your emotions run amuck. They will often sabotage the outcome you want. Take control of your words.

Instead of being your own worst enemy, be your own best friend. Stop sabotaging the goals you want. Think before you react. It is critical to a fulfilled life.

Now, look at your best friend in the mirror and tell her why, "I like myself right now because _____, I love my life right now because _____. Don't forget to add your celebration!

DAY 17: SABOTAGING YOURSELF

Check the box when you are done:

☐ I like myself (3x)

☐ I love my life (3x)

Congratulate yourself for attacking your negative behaviors. Go and enjoy right now!

Day 18:
Supporting Others

Remember how you held the mirror in front of you and you couldn't see anyone except yourself and your past? Well, move the mirror a little and see that there are other people out there. And they need your help. After you help others, you will see a much happier face in your mirror.

If you have been focusing on yourself, then it is time to look at something else: focus on helping others. When you focus on someone else's need, you can forget about yourself and all that you perceive wrong with you and your life!

What do you like to do? You don't have to be an expert. There are many areas where you can help others. What are your interests, skills, and goals? What causes are important to you? You don't have to dive into committing to hours of volunteering. You can start small.

When I helped start a soup kitchen in our town, I believed in the need. However, I was uncomfortable with being around people, any group of people. So, I worked behind the scenes, organizing food deliveries and donations, assisting in food preparation, and

DAY 18: SUPPORTING OTHERS

washing dishes. It was years later before I took time to get to know the guests who came in. I wrote my first book, Miracles Among Us, about the guests and volunteers at the Lebanon Soup Kitchen. I felt blessed that individuals shared their often-heart-breaking stories with me. I have watched other stories play out in real-time. Some ended sadly, some ended in success. My life has been changed by my experience, and I can also say that I have positively affected other people's lives.

Have you ever felt insignificant? Not anymore. Do you like to sew? Do yard work? Work with wood? Groom dogs? Paint? There are many ways you can give to your community.

Check with the local Chamber of Commerce for a list of nonprofits that rely on volunteers. Helping others can put things in perspective. There are many people in need of basic assistance. By engaging in your community, you can see a bigger picture.

Do you like watching young minds explore new things? Ask at the local school. You could mentor a child in reading or math. Or just be a friend.

4-H programs provide many opportunities in different fields to volunteer with youth. If you don't consider yourself a teacher, then demonstrate what you know how to do.

Do you like sports? Local Boys and Girls Club are often needing help.

It doesn't have to be an organized program. Help a neighbor with their yard work or take them shopping. If you like to garden, share your produce. If you like to cook or bake, share your creations with shut-ins. Donate a craft. Teach a skill. Think outside the usual. You can find a way.

Opportunities are only limited to your imagination. You can make a difference in someone's life by offering just a little of yourself. What is holding you back? Maybe self-sabotage? Worrying you are not good enough? Would the people there like me? Nonsense. You are a capable adult. People will like you when you treat them as you want to be treated. Climb out of your shell. You can take tiny steps, but get going.

You might not change the world, but you can make their world a better place. Even if you help one person, you have succeeded.

Have you noticed this is an upward spiral? The more you reach out to others, the happier you are. You are wired to want to help others. It makes you happy. The more you feel happy, the more you want to do what makes you happy. While you are helping others, you may reduce your stress or depression. And along the way, you may make new friendships.

Finding places to volunteer is easy in most communities. Go on-line, lookup community centers, service organizations, hospitals, schools, or check with your local Chamber of Commerce. Volunteering can make you a vital part of someone's life. And that's a great feeling. Have fun with new adventures.

Look in the mirror and tell your best friend about your plans to help someone. Say to her, "I like myself right now because _____, I love my life right now because _____.

DAY 18: SUPPORTING OTHERS

Check the box when you are done:

- ☐ I like myself (3x)
- ☐ I love my life (3x)

Go and celebrate your joy with others!

Day 19:

Gratitude

What are you grateful for? Most people answer quickly with "family and friends." And those are great answers. Relationships are an essential part of your life. Do you appreciate those in your life that bring you laughter or smiles? Have you told them how they affect you? "Gratitude is the healthiest of all human emotions. The more you express gratitude for what you have, the more likely you will have even more to express gratitude for." Zig Ziglar

It is not just having gratitude but also expressing gratitude that increases your happiness. It is one of those upward spirals. You receive and are thankful, so you give. It may be giving back to the one who gave to you, passing the generosity on to someone else, or taking action to improve yourself or your situation. When you act upon your sentiment of appreciating someone or something, you can see more things to be thankful for.

Say your neighbor gives you a bucket of apples from her tree because she knows you like to bake. There are more apples than you can use, so you make an extra pie to give back to her, plus you make applesauce for the boy across the street who mowed your lawn.

DAY 19: GRATITUDE

"In daily life, we must see that it is not happiness that makes us grateful, but gratefulness that makes us happy." Joshua Becker, author of **The More of Less** and **The Minimalist Home**.

The greatest thing to be thankful for is life itself. We were given life for only a short period. Do you appreciate every day and make the best of it?

When I took a bottle of pills to rid myself of pain, did I appreciate life? Not hardly. I focused on what I considered bad and did not know how to enjoy what I did have. Yes, I could blame it on the way I was raised. But I have had decades to figure out just how precious life is and how I could make it better. I regret the years I wasted worrying about how I looked to others. I am here to give you guidelines on how to take control of your life and enjoy it right now.

Find one thing that you are genuinely grateful for. Your husband? Children? House? Job? What is important to you? How would you feel if that was taken from your life? Think about it. Would you feel devastated? Then now is the time to be grateful for it. How do you treat something so precious? I hope you aren't taking it for granted.

When was the last time you gave a compliment? Did you thank your husband for scraping ice from the windshield this morning? Did you tell your kids you were proud of how they treated their peers? Have you ever told your boss or co-workers that you appreciated their support in your job? There are so many things to be thankful for.

Society proclaims that you can't be satisfied unless you have just one more thing. Materialism is the most significant barrier to being grateful. If you are thankful for what you have, chances are you will care for that item and enjoy it while spending less time and energy seeking more things. Do empty promises commonly seen in ads influence you to purchase more? Probably not.

You have a blank screen in front of you called today. Each morning you can wake up and intentionally choose to be thankful for the new day given you. Your choices from the moment you wake up will shape how you feel, think, and act during the day. If you fill that first moment with gratitude, you can go forward with optimism and make the kind of day you want.

"Sing and make music in your heart to the Lord, always giving thanks to God the Father for everything, in the name of our Lord Jesus Christ" (Ephesians 5:20). When you have a joyful heart, you may feel more like singing and expressing the joy it brings.

How do you build up your gratitude? You start by focusing on what you do have, not what you want. Do you overlook the small things, which really aren't small things? Such as sight? Hearing? Your ability to walk? Sing? Ride horses?

I used to love riding horses. I enjoyed the trail-rides in the mountains or along the beach. I gained confidence in myself showing my horse in reining. It meant so much. But then my muscles began breaking down. My balance was off-kilter. I felt exhausted after only a little exercise. I needed help to ride, even for short periods. I tried pushing my abilities, but after I collapsed in the field one day, I chose to accept my limitations. My heart ached.

DAY 19: GRATITUDE

Yes, there is still sadness in not being able to jump on my horse whenever I want. But I am grateful that God has made my life meaningful. I still cherish all the memories of riding. My mission has changed from trying to make myself happy to passionately wanting to help others feel more accepting and loving of themselves.

I probably wouldn't have found this new path in my life if I had been able to continue all my outdoor activities. While I was bed-ridden, I focused on God, His Word, and talking with Him about everything. I am so thankful for the relationship that cultivated and where He has led me.

What are you grateful for in this gift called life? Tell others how much you appreciate them. Give compliments whenever possible. Look for the good in everything. And that includes you. Pick up your mirror and tell your best friend all that you are thankful for. Tell her, "I like myself right now because _____, I love my life right now because _____."

Check the box when you are done:

☐ I like myself (3x)

☐ I love my life (3x)

Go and enjoy right now! Be thankful throughout the day and repeat, "I like myself...

Day 20:

Design Your Future

What are your plans for your future? Have you decided on a path, or are you waiting around to see what comes up? I guarantee nothing is going to arrive at your door and present your fantasy life to you.

The decisions you make today will decide where you are tomorrow. If you are not working toward a goal, you won't reach one.

Are you having a hard time knowing where to begin? Well, let's start with your fantasy. Close your eyes for a moment. Shut everything and everyone out. Take a deep, relaxing breath. Before you step into your dream, let me explain. There is nothing in your way of reaching your goal. You have all the money, all the information, and all the support you need. No one is in your way. Dream what you want. No saying, "If only so-and-so would do this." Remember, they aren't in the picture.

Now, with everything out of your way, what would you like your life to look like? Do you want to stay in the same area? Move to a tropical island? Be honest and realistic. What do you want to be doing? Do you

DAY 20: DESIGN YOUR FUTURE

want a career? A house and car? Who do you want around you?

Imagine a setting where you will be happy and enjoying your life. Write it all down. Are you single or married? Do you have kids? Grandkids? It is your dream. Make it all you want.

What will it take to get there? Let's work backward from your dream to the present. If you want a career, what will it take to build one? To have that job you really want, you may need to get some education. So, what is stopping you?

Education costs money. You may need transportation or a computer or both. Is money the reason you are hindered? Do you have a job where you can save a little at a time? If so, how much have you saved?

If you don't have a job but need one, have you looked?

This is the beginning of your plan. You need a job to earn money, pay bills and attend college. Are you taking steps to do either?

You can't focus on that house in the country or penthouse apartment until you examine the steps right in front of you. You can't reach the top rung without stepping on the bottom one.

If you are not moving forward with what you can do today, you are not working toward your goal. Read back through this book. Do you know your value? Are you focusing on positive solutions and self-talk? Have you peeled your old labels and set realistic expectations? Accepting how your past fits in but doesn't define your life is essential. Have you forgiven others? Are you working on the issues from the other chapters?

Having the lifestyle you want does not come easy. It takes planning and consistent hard work. Your perspective of yourself and the world around you will play a part in how well you move forward. It will depend on who you allow into your life. We need people. We need companionship, encouragement, and help. But who you surround yourself with will make a difference on where you are headed. Are you with the people you want to be like? Or are you spending your time with people who hold you back?

What do you and your friends talk about when together? Are you complaining about a boss, a neighbor, a friend, or each other? How are you going to get rid of your negative self-talk if you are talking negatively about others? Do they encourage you to pursue your dream, or do they point out all the obstacles?

Do you have people who will encourage and support you? That may be a teacher, counselor, or someone you met at church or a service organization. If you are happy with your life just the way it is, you probably wouldn't be reading this book.

The best way to make decisions and plans is to ask our Lord about them. He has a vested interest in you because you are His creation, and He loves you. "For we are God's workmanship, created in Christ Jesus to do good work..." (Ephesians 2:10). You are created to do good. You are created to succeed. But you don't have to do it alone. He says He will be with you. If you have never confessed your sins, your brokenness, and asked Jesus into your life, you can do it now. He will

DAY 20: DESIGN YOUR FUTURE

forgive you and be with you through whatever you decide.

Pick up your mirror and feel that happy-dance inside, say, "I like myself right now because _____, I love my life right now because _____."

Check the box when you are done:

☐ I like myself (3x)

☐ I love my life (3x)

Go and enjoy right now! Celebrate the fabulous future you are working toward!

Day 21:

Sow into Your Life

What are you planting in your life today that you can harvest in your future? To sow means to plant or scatter seeds with the purpose of growth. The idea that any farmer or gardener will attest to is that you harvest what you sow. The harvest cannot be different than the type of seed planted. That is true in your life also.

"Do not be deceived; God cannot be mocked. A man reaps what he sows. The one who sows to please his sinful nature, from that nature will reap destruction, the one who sows to please the Spirit, from the Spirit will reap eternal life. Let us not become weary in doing good, for at the proper time we will reap a harvest if we do not give up" (Galatians 6:7-9).

Are you sowing the type of life you want to live? Was your ultimate dream to do what you are doing today? Chances are you have dreams for your future. I have a sign that says, "Don't ever let your memories be greater than your dreams." Never stop dreaming.

Remember Day 3? Are you sowing into positive or negative energy? Positive breeds positive just as neg-

DAY 21: SOW INTO YOUR LIFE

ative breeds' negative. You reap what you put in. If you speak in negative ways, you will feel negative. If your expectations are that you will fail, that is what will happen.

It is just as true with being positive. If you sow into others with encouragement and help, you will harvest the same. If you are sowing into your community by helping others when they are in need, you can expect rewards in the area of belonging, being connected, and relationships.

If you know Jesus as your Lord and Savior, you can positively know that He is with you throughout the rest of your life, plus eternity. That is a reason for you to be thankful and positive every day. He loves you unconditionally, and He knows your heart, your thoughts, and your motives.

The choice is yours. Every day you make thousands of choices—some more crucial than others. Be mindful of what you allow in your thoughts. *"Finally, brothers, whatever is true, whatever is noble, whatever is right, whatever is admirable–if anything is excellent or praiseworthy-think about such things"* (Philippians 4:8).

To take control of your life, you must take control of your thoughts.

The one thing I regret about my life is that I didn't learn to enjoy it earlier. I have had so many experiences that were fun, exciting, rewarding, or challenging. They were all experienced through a fog of anxiety and doubt. That fog was only lifted when I fully saw who God said I was and who I could be. I believe in myself because my Creator believes in me.

Each day you said one thing you liked about yourself and one thing you loved about your life. Write them down. Post them where you will see them. Reinforce your attitude by memorizing your list. You can begin your new journey to enjoying right now.

Pick up your mirror. Read your list to your best friend. Do you feel better about that person than you did 21 days ago? Have you learned ways to encourage your best friend? Or to sow into what you want out of each day. Fill your day with positive energy and keep growing.

Have you perfected your celebration moves? Don't forget how important it is for you to celebrate. Did your gestures grow along with you? Look at that lovely face in the mirror and say, "I like myself right now because _____, I love my life right now because _____.

Check the box when you are done:

☐ I like myself (3x)

☐ I love my life (3x)

Go and enjoy right now!

Congratulations!! You made it! I am proud of you. My wish for you is that you love yourself with the same love that Jesus has for you. Celebrate your life! You go, Girl!

Congratulations! You made it through 21 days of examining yourself. You're not done. Your journey is just beginning. How will you apply each day's lessons? They are only effective when you put them to work in

DAY 21: SOW INTO YOUR LIFE

your life. Reading is the first part. You need to be aware how the daily topic is manifesting in your life. When you see it and accept it, in order to remember it, you need to take action. Make looking in the mirror and saying, "I like myself right now because..." a daily habit. You have been doing it for 21 days. Continue it until you mean it. Then, you will enjoy finding ways to finish the sentence.

You now know that you have value. Let that motivate you to forgive anyone who may have hurt you and to put your past behind. Look for ways to encourage yourself with self-talk. Surround yourself with a positive atmosphere, including the people you allow in your life. Set boundaries and don't accept false labels others may try to paste on you. Give of yourself and help others. Sow into a positive, upward spiral and enjoy the ride.

If you put the book down and continue living the way you always have, you will get the same results. And you probably wouldn't be reading this if you were happy with your life. You can move toward being happier and enjoying your life if you apply the knowledge.

Read over all the chapters whenever needed to remind yourself what you can do, then do it. Liking yourself and loving your life is not a destination. It is a lifestyle. Sure, there are times you may take a step backwards. But that is part of the journey. Keep moving forward.

Now, you need to take action. Believe in yourself and take care of yourself! That is not a luxury. It is a necessity! Go and be thankful for your life every day.

Tell Me All About It

I'm So Glad We Had This Time Together!

Thank you so much for joining me on this 21-Day Journey. I pray it was a blessing to you. If so, may I ask a quick favor? It would mean so much to me. And it would help other women find their way to this important message.

Can you take just a few minutes to write a quick review? Now don't let that word scare you. It's really just sharing a short testimony of how God has used this book in your life.

You can go to www.NanceyWest.com/review

Thanks so much for doing that. It really means a lot to me as an author. I'm going to look in the mirror and say, "I love my life right now because someone just wrote a nice review for me!" Here comes my happy dance!

You're Invited

I'd love to get to know you better!

That's why YOU are invited to join my special Facebook Group

https://www.facebook.com/groups/likingmyselflovingmylife

You can also register for my free 3-Day "Revealing the Very Best You" Online Bootcamp. Just visit www.LikingMyself.com

Looking forward to celebrating with you.

Blessings,
Nancey West

Special Thanks

I want to especially thank my husband, who has supported me through years of learning the lessons I write about. And my children, who grew up to be astonishing adults.

Thanks to Cindy Ongers, who has been my cheerleader and who has introduced me to many amazing people to enrich my life.

My appreciation to Paula Newman, who has been my mentor in spiritual growth.

Then, there are many counselors who I do not remember but left me with many nuggets of truth to apply to my life.

And to all the women who have come to the Lebanon Soup Kitchen. I saw my younger self in their desperate eyes and longed to help them see who they were truly meant to be. I hope you find peace.

Resources

National Suicide Prevention Lifeline
1-800-273-TALK (8255)

American Psychological Association Answer Center
1-888-35-PSYCH (77924)

National Institute of Mental Health
www.nimh.nih.gov

National Alliance on Mental Illness
www.nami.org

National Crisis Text Line
Text "go" to 741 741

Veteran Crisis Line
800-273-8255 press 1

Veteran Crisis Text Line
838255

To look for resources in your area
Cal 2-1-1
https//call-211.org/

ABOUT THE AUTHOR

Nancey is an author and speaker. After a lifetime of dealing with depression and anxiety, she is now living at peace with who she is. Her passion is teaching women that it's possible to go from feeling worthless to knowing they are priceless.

Nancey is active in her church and community, reaching out to at-risk youth and adults. She is the co-founder and former chairman of an active soup kitchen ministry. She is certified in mental health first aid.

She and her husband own and operate a Christmas tree farm in the foothills of the Cascade Mountains in Oregon. They have two children and two grandchildren.

She enjoys spending time with family and friends and experiencing the wonders of the great outdoors.

merlinhelp@cornell.edu